THE LOST CASINO

Where Every Choice Counts

PRIYANKA

ISBN
Paperback 979-8-89699-912-6
Hardcase 979-8-89724-790-5

"uddhared ātmanātmānaṁ nātmānam avasādayet
ātmaiva hyātmano bandhur ātmaiva ripur ātmanaḥ"

– Bhagavad Gita Verse 6.5

Contents

From The Author's Heart

"I planned, and I planned….., then life took over".

On a beautiful day, I boldly declared my intention to the Universe: to write my first book. I envisioned myself as a 'woman on a mission,' completing my book in a fervent burst of inspiration over sleepless nights. However, six months later, the inspiration I had hoped for was still out of reach. Finally, I took my pen and convinced myself to take the first step. I had no clear idea of what I wanted to write, but my mind was brimming with unspoken thoughts, eager for a literary outlet.

Hesitantly, I began, unaware that the year 2024 would be a year of transformation, marked by uncertainty but guided by an unshakable faith that the dots would connect. And they did, in ways more extraordinary than I could have imagined. All the events in my life unfolded seamlessly, as though orchestrated by an unseen hand. Reflecting on these events, I am convinced of the role of divine grace. This invisible force transforms ordinary events into extraordinary outcomes, much like a simple offering becomes sacred when touched by divinity.

This book explores the intricate connection between human behaviour and the deeper currents beneath the surface. I invite you to reflect on your life and be aware of the unseen forces shaping your journey. Let the book serve as both a mirror and a guide to seeing your world—and yourself—with new eyes.

Happy Insightful Reading!

Introduction

What drives us to risk everything for a chance at something more?

It is a question that echoes in the allure of a casino—a space that symbolises chance, risk-taking, and the promise of winning big. Here, grand dreams and aspirations come to life, fuelled by the illusion of control in a world of chance.

Like a casino, life is a dynamic interplay of chance, strategy, and resolve. Every choice we make—whether a leap of faith or a calculated move—is akin to placing a bet on the unpredictable table of existence. Yet, within this vast array of possibilities, we all face 'lost casino moments'—the times when hesitation, fear, or self-doubt keeps us from playing to our fullest potential, and we lose sight of our capacity for transformation and growth.

And yet, the "lost casino" is not without its potential. These moments of uncertainty—our casino moments—are not failures but profound invitations. They challenge us to see beyond the surface, embrace life's unpredictability, and approach every decision with resolve, courage, and an open heart. By confronting and understanding the "lost casino" in our lives, we gain the clarity to reclaim our dreams and move closer to winning the ultimate jackpot of fulfillment and purpose.

Welcome to _The Lost Casino_! Let us embark on this journey of self-discovery, resilience, and transformation. In the silence of choices, let the game begin.

Chapter One

Live Like An Insect

"You are living like an insect! Totally useless!" roared the exasperated father. His 15-year-old son stood at the door, head bowed, as though lifting his gaze would further cement the comparison. On discreet inquiry, I learned that the father's anger stemmed from his son's refusal to man the family shop after school, choosing instead to play football with friends. The boy's mediocre performance in his recent school exams aggravated the situation.

This incident stayed with me. During a weekly meet-up with friends, I brought it up. Reactions varied. Some empathised with the father, citing today's youth as irresponsible and inconsiderate of their parents' struggles. When I asked, "Are we living like insects?" the responses intrigued me. One friend adamantly declared, "Definitely not! I live with full consciousness." Another friend interpreted the father's words symbolically, suggesting he meant his son was wasting his potential, living a lowly existence akin to an insect's survival-driven life. After a round of intense discussions, we concluded that, from a human perspective, insects symbolise a lack of higher goals or consciousness.

The phrase "live like an insect" lingered in my mind, causing discomfort. Not because I felt solidarity with insects but because it challenged my assumptions. Humans are often described as "divine beings having an earthly existence," placed at the apex of the living order due to our capacity for reasoning, judgment, and decision-making. Insects, by contrast, seem instinct-driven and survival-focused.

One gloomy day, I was weighed down by self-doubt, so I decided to take a walk in the park. The air was cool, and it was peaceful all around. As I walked past a patch of flowers, something caught my eye—a tiny bee flitting from one flower to another. It seemed unbothered by the world's chaos, intent on its singular mission of gathering nectar. I stopped and watched it for a while, curious about its unrelenting focus.

What struck me was how the bee approached its task. It did not linger too long on one flower or ignore the smaller blossoms. Every flower seemed to matter. Each interaction was purposeful, contributing to something greater than itself. At that moment, it was not just collecting nectar; it was unknowingly enabling pollination—a process that would lead to the blooming of new life, sustaining ecosystems far beyond its understanding.

The simplicity of its act felt profound. It was not burdened by existential doubt or the need for validation. It performed its role with quiet persistence. It simply did what it was designed to do, and in doing so, it became an integral part of the grander scheme of things. Watching it, I thought about the times I had questioned whether my contributions mattered, fearing they were too small to make a difference. Yet, here was this tiny bee, showing me that every action had a ripple effect, no matter how small.

I sat on a nearby bench, reflecting on the lesson the bee had silently imparted. It is not the scale of our actions but the sincerity and intention behind them that define impact. Whether helping a friend, offering a kind word, or pursuing a dream, each effort contributes to a greater purpose—even if we cannot immediately perceive its effect. That day, I walked away with a lighter heart. The bee's action gave me the insight to focus on the process rather than the outcome and to trust that my efforts, however small, were part of something larger than myself.

Bees thrive by living in sync with their design. Their singular objective—to gather nectar and make honey—fulfills a purpose beyond their comprehension. Bees are not plagued by insecurity or jealousy. They do not compare their nectar collection with other bees or question the flowers' approval. They live their purpose. What higher goals does the bee need to thrive in line with the design of the Creator? Have we ever heard of a bee waking up in the morning and saying, "Today I am full of self-doubt; I cannot collect nectar"? Or perhaps a bee complaining to other bees, "The flowers do not like me; they are envious of me."

Insects live in harmony with their species, demonstrating social skills and resilience to survive in their environment. What greater goal can there be than this? We human beings, as evolved creatures, are designed to live joyfully and with full consciousness. Yet, what do we do? We burden ourselves with self-doubt, envy, fear, and guilt, chasing fulfillment in external achievements while forgetting our innate peace. In our quest for accomplishments and supremacy, we disrupt equilibrium, leading to many a man-made disaster.

What do we mean when we say insects have low consciousness? Consciousness is not something easily defined or measured. It is not a concept that words can fully capture, for it transcends language. Our biases and beliefs shape every attempt to describe it. The terms "high consciousness" and "low consciousness" are constructs of the duality in the human mind. Perhaps, instead of ranking consciousness as high or low, we might recognise it as present in all living beings and view it as a universal thread connecting all life.

Let us take an example. Imagine buying an electric iron and a refrigerator, each designed to operate with a specific voltage. Do we ever question why the refrigerator's voltage is unsuitable for the electric iron, or vice versa? Just as each appliance is built to function optimally with a particular set of specifications, so are insects designed to live and function harmoniously with their unique purpose and environment.

When a bee collects nectar and contributes to the honey-making process, it does so with what we might call 'bee-consciousness'—a state of being that does not need to align with 'human consciousness'. A bee finds fulfillment not by comparing itself to other bees but by simply living out its purpose. It does not measure its success by the amount of nectar it gathers compared to its fellow bees, nor does it worry about tomorrow's flowers or the approval of its hive. It lives entirely in the present, embracing its role. In contrast, though we are designed for joyful, conscious living, our fulfillment is often tied to relative achievements, measured against the success of others. We carry an invisible measuring stick, constantly comparing ourselves to those around us.

The father's statement, "You are living like an insect", reflects this tendency to compare—yet in this case, the comparison is with insects, not other humans. Was the father's disappointment born out of genuine concern, or did societal pressures and his fears shape it? I wonder if any insect parent has ever told its offspring, "You are behaving like a human. Strive to be like an insect."

Every being exists for a reason, designed differently but purposefully. An insect does not need human-like goals to thrive; it fulfills its role by being itself. No other lofty goal is required. To live as an insect is its destiny, perfectly in sync with the Universe's design - nothing more, nothing less. Is living like an insect—

doing what we are designed to do with intention and focus—an insult, or could it be a profound compliment? In his anger, did the father fail to see the potential in his son's individuality—just as we often overlook the significance of an insect's existence?

To "live like an insect" is not to shrink into insignificance but to live with simplicity, focus, and alignment with our true purpose and as per the blueprint of the Universe. This is uplifting in itself. From an insect's life, we can find a profound lesson: survival is not about size but resilience and synchronicity with the world around us. Perhaps, in their silent consonance with the Universe, insects are closer to the divine design than we, with all our chaotic pursuits, ever will be.

How can we shift our perspective and find a deeper connection with the natural flow of life?

Chapter Two
Dice With Five Sides

"**A**unty, pleeze play wit me," said my friend's three-year-old son. I had been playing with him for the past hour, seeking him out as he hid behind the sofa. After the tenth round, I was sure I could find him even in my dreams. Small children have a unique way of engaging with play—they never seem to tire of it, their excitement remaining fresh long after adults have wearied.

"No," I said firmly. "Now we will read a book. Please show me your storybooks." He looked at me briefly and, without a word, toddled off to fetch his books. When he returned, he held up one and said, "Pleeze read dis". Relieved to rest my legs, I gladly agreed.

The story he had chosen was titled *The Frog in the Well and the Bull*. Its content went somewhat like this:

Once upon a time, a frog lived in a small, dark well. Content with his life, he believed the well was the largest and best place in the world. One sunny day, another frog from the nearby fields hopped into the well to drink water. The field-frog looked around and thought about how small and confined the well was compared to the vast fields he lived in. He tried to explain the expansive world outside to the well-frog, full of open spaces, lush greenery, and creatures much larger than anything the well-frog could imagine, including a mighty bull. The well-frog could not fathom anything more significant than his well or himself.

Determined to prove his superiority, he began puffing himself up, trying to match the size of the bull described by the field frog. He inflated himself bigger and bigger, ignoring his body's limits. In his stubbornness and pride, he kept going until he finally burst. The field-frog, saddened by the well-frog's demise, hopped away, reflecting on how ignorance and arrogance can lead to one's downfall.

After hearing the story, the little boy puffed up his chest, mimicking the frog with playful enthusiasm. I could not help but laugh at his innocence. Later, I said goodbye to him, leaving with a promise to return the next day for another game of hide-and-seek. Though sorrowful, he waved goodbye with an utterly refreshing innocence. Spending time with him lifted my spirits. The purity and simplicity with which children engage with the world reminded me of a time when life was simpler and less complicated.

When I returned home, I received a call from my daughter, who was away at her Institute. Her voice, usually filled with enthusiasm, now sounded dejected and strained. "I don't know what to do", she began, her words tumbling out in a rush. "There are so many activities I could join, but I can't decide which ones to participate in. If I choose one, I'll have to give up another, and I'm afraid I'll regret it. It feels like I am rolling a die with five sides—each choice leading to a different outcome, and I don't know which side will bring the right result. I am trying to prioritise, but I am being pulled in a million directions. If I don't get into this one thing, then so-and-so won't happen, and I'll miss out. But at the same time, I want this other thing to happen, and I don't know how to make it all fit. What if I make the wrong choice? I want to get it right, but everything feels so overwhelming." Her voice trembled slightly. I could hear the burden of her doubt, the pressure of trying to balance everything, and the fear of making the wrong decision.

Her words carried the weight of many young people's dilemmas—the overwhelming abundance of choices and the fear of making the wrong one. Her Institute offered the option of joining various clubs, ranging from technical to cultural, and each demanded significant time and effort. It was natural for her to feel the pressure. I listened patiently, offering gentle advice: "Choose the activities that align with your long-term goals. Remember, you cannot do everything at once."

As I hung up, I reflected on a phrase that had shaped much of my upbringing: *Where there is a will, there is a way.* While this mantra has inspired countless individuals to push their limits, it can also create an unnecessary mental strain. The issue arises when we define ourselves solely by our ability to will things into existence, as though sheer determination should always guarantee success. When roadblocks appear or outcomes fall short of our expectations, we often end up unfairly labelling ourselves as weak-willed or inadequate. This mindset overlooks the complexity of life's challenges and the value of resilience, patience, and adaptability, equally essential in navigating the path to fulfillment.

My daughter's dilemma reminded me of how often we become trapped in believing every decision must be perfect, as if our 'will' alone determines success. We place so much pressure on ourselves to get it right, fearing that any misstep will lead to failure. But what if the best outcomes do not come from rigid control or relentless striving? What if they arise instead from trusting the unfolding of life, allowing ourselves to be guided by its natural flow, and facing the uncertainties along the way? Sometimes, significant success comes not from forcing our will upon the world but from surrendering to the process and remaining open to its unexpected possibilities.

The story of the well-frog came to mind. Are we humans not often like the well-frog? When we insist that life should unfold according to our limited perspectives, are we not puffing ourselves up with a sense of control that is ultimately illusory? Are we not confining ourselves to the narrow well of our desires, ignoring the vast possibilities beyond?

Our belief in the supremacy of our will often blinds us to a fundamental truth: everything in nature is interconnected. We are not isolated beings operating independently of the Universe. We are deeply embedded within it. Our survival depends on the sun, air, water, and the Earth's ecosystem. This interconnectedness means that while we are part of the Universe, the Universe is also a part of us, much like the ocean and the waves. A wave is part of the ocean, but the ocean is also part of the wave. Waves cannot exist without the ocean, and their movements reflect the ocean's essence.

To understand this intrinsic relation between us and the Universe, let us consider the process of photosynthesis in plants. The sunlight that fuels this process is the same energy that sustains us, as we rely on plants for oxygen and nourishment. The air we breathe, made up of elements like oxygen and carbon dioxide, has been circulating on Earth for millions of years, exchanged by plants, animals, and even the oceans. In this way, we are not just passive recipients of the Universe's offerings but active participants in an ongoing exchange cycle.

On a more personal level, when we feel at peace in Nature, such as when walking in a forest or gazing at the stars, we experience this connection. The serenity we feel is not just a response to the beauty around us but a recognition that we, too, are part of the same cosmic dance. This deep connection underscores that the Universe and we are indivisible, each affecting the other profoundly.

When we understand this, we can begin to let go of the need to control every outcome. Instead of resisting situations or forcing them to fit our limited perspectives, we can accept life's unfolding. Each challenge presents an opportunity to expand our horizons and discover new possibilities. The story of the well-frog serves as a poignant reminder: when we confine ourselves to the well of our limited understanding, we risk missing out on the vastness of life. Instead of draining our energy and trying to mould situations to fit our expectations, we can trust the Universe to unfurl in ways far beyond our imagination. We often view our 'will' as the sole driver of success, forgetting that life unravels within a vast web of interconnectedness, where our desires are just one thread in a larger tapestry.

As I mulled over these thoughts, the little boy's innocent laughter and the well-frog's tale merged in my mind. I remembered my daughter's words, "I feel as if I am rolling a die with five sides". She has unwittingly articulated a profound truth in her innocence, cutting straight to the heart of the matter with remarkable clarity. Life, after all, is like dice with five sides—unpredictable, multifaceted, and endlessly intriguing. All we need is the courage to roll it and the wisdom to embrace whatever comes up.

Are we ready to roll the five-sided dice of life, trusting that each outcome, no matter how unpredictable, holds the potential for growth and discovery?

Chapter Three

The Sinister Otter

The other day, I was invited to a birthday party for a one-year-old. The venue, a charming resort, was beautifully decorated for the occasion. I knew the mother well and a few of her relatives. I reached on time, only to find that many guests had not yet arrived. The mother greeted me warmly, thanking me for attending the party. Since I was early, I could explore the place, and we had some quiet time to chat. I asked her how life was treating her and whether she was enjoying motherhood. Her face lit up as she spoke of her baby being a blessing in her life. But almost immediately, her expression clouded. She admitted that her husband had not changed much and that she was trying to adjust for the baby's sake. Before we could delve deeper, other guests arrived, and our conversation remained unfinished.

As the party progressed, the designated photographer moved around, capturing moments. I observed the father of the baby greeting guests warmly and posing for photos with his wife and the baby. On the surface, they seemed like any other normal couple. The atmosphere was warm, with relatives from both sides mingling, though her family seemed to linger in the background, leaving the spotlight to his side.

During lunch, I found myself seated next to the baby's maternal Aunt. A casual conversation led me to comment that things seemed to have improved between the couple. My remark stemmed from my knowledge that, two years earlier, their marriage had nearly collapsed, with both sides considering divorce. The Aunt wistfully smiled and said, "That's the problem—he behaves differently with others and differently with her."

The Aunt's words lingered in my mind. It is not uncommon for people to project different personas in different settings. We often mask our true feelings, presenting an image consistent with the expectations of the external world. Yet, this duality can be more pronounced in some individuals, leading to a stark contrast between their public and private selves.

This reflection brought to mind the otter, a semi-aquatic mammal known for its playful, curious, and adaptable nature. The connection with otters likely surfaced because I watched a TV documentary about them just a few days ago. Otters are social creatures, sliding down mudbanks and playing with objects in the water, and their playfulness is thought to foster social bonding and learning. However, imagine an otter that hides a sinister nature beneath its playful exterior. Would it not change how we see them? Such an anomaly would disrupt our perception of otters as harmless, fun-loving creatures, replacing trust with suspicion.

Just as this 'imagined otter' challenges our expectations, we encounter similar inconsistencies in the human world. There are 'sinister otters' in the human world—individuals who appear charming and harmless but conceal calculating or harmful tendencies. They present themselves as approachable and trustworthy, gaining others' confidence, only to exploit it for personal gain. If we reflect, we will find that sometime in our lives, we may all have encountered someone whose outward charm left us questioning their true intentions.

At first glance, being a 'sinister otter' might seem advantageous. Such individuals can manipulate situations to their benefit, maintaining a polished exterior while masking their true nature. However, this duality comes at a cost. The gap between the inner and outer selves is narrow at the beginning of their journey to build a façade. With ever-increasing practice and mastery in various situations, the gap widens, making authentic relationships nearly impossible. Over time, maintaining such a deceptive persona demands effort and careful manipulation.

For example, let us consider a person who is 'gentle and encouraging' with friends and colleagues but 'critical and unappreciative' toward family. Now, which is their true self? Since real selves often emerge in non-threatening situations, the critical and unappreciative self may reflect their dominant nature. To conceal their true nature and shield their external relationships, the 'sinister otter' must vigilantly maintain their false display. This constant effort results in superficial connections and isolation, even when surrounded by acquaintances. While the pretence may yield short-term gains like influence, status, or resources, it ultimately leads to long-term consequences of distrust and alienation.

This sinister otter's 'critical and unappreciative behaviour' often arises from a deep struggle of self-acceptance. When we fail to accept ourselves, we project this dissatisfaction onto those around us. Their criticism of their family members reflects their inner turmoil. They carry heavy emotional baggage, often invisible to the outside world. This baggage includes unresolved insecurities, fear of rejection, and an overwhelming need for validation. Over time, the effort to maintain a false persona takes a toll, leading to stress, anxiety, and a fractured sense of identity. The internal conflict between their exterior and true self prevents them from forming authentic bonds, and they feel isolated, even when surrounded by people.

This concept is not limited to others. At times, it can reflect aspects of our own journey. There can even be a 'sinister otter' within each of us, ready to emerge if we are unaware. When we are under the influence of this 'sinister otter', we mask our true intentions and emotions behind a veneer of charm, playfulness, or harmlessness while pursuing self-serving goals or manipulating situations for personal gain. For instance, we might appear as team players at work, offering help and support while quietly competing for recognition or advancement. In relationships, we might present ourselves as caring and loving while subtly undermining our partner's confidence or manipulating them to suit our needs. While this may yield short-term gains, it creates emotional and relational fissures. The eventual exposure of our true intentions often leads to a breakdown of trust, damaged relationships, and profound internal conflict.

Recognising the 'sinister otter' within us is the first step toward change. It requires honesty and introspection to understand the root causes of our behaviour and the courage to stop the masquerade. This journey is essential for building authentic connections with others and finding inner peace. The first and most crucial step is acknowledging the inner demon that fuels this behaviour. We must confront the inadequacies, self-doubt, and anxiety that drive us to construct a charade. This self-awareness is the foundation of transformation. This is the point where we stop justifying our actions and accept the truth about our behaviours and intentions. We start confronting the beliefs we have been carrying: the need to appear flawless, the fear of being judged, and the discomfort with vulnerability.

Narrowing the gap between who we are and who we project ourselves to be is not an overnight process. It requires consistent effort, self-compassion, and a commitment to authenticity.

However, this journey is worth the effort, as it leads to meaningful connections, genuine relationships, and a sense of inner peace that cannot coexist with the constant stress of maintaining a deceptive front.

As I left the party that day, I could not help but wonder how many 'sinister otters' hide in plain sight, struggling with their masks. The Aunt's words echoed in my mind: "He behaves differently with her." They served as a reminder that true transformation begins with honesty—first with ourselves, then with others.

How often do we hide behind facades, and what would it take to begin our own journey of authenticity?

Chapter Four

The Unbalanced Plank

"Come along with me; you will enjoy it," insisted my friend. "Ok, let me think about it," I said, not intending to think about it. The matter of discussion was a four-day upcoming holiday. She was planning to visit her distant relatives for two days. They lived in a village around 300 kilometres from our city. Since I had no other plans, she coaxed me to accompany her. I was hesitant. For one, I did not want to put the relatives in discomfort by suddenly landing there; secondly, I was unsure whether I would be comfortable. But my friend was one step ahead of me. She said she had already spoken to her relatives, who assured her they would happily host me. That settled the matter. From the satisfactory grin on her face, I saw that she was glad to have her way.

On the first day of our holiday, we started our trip early in the morning to avoid traffic. After driving for some time, we stopped at a small roadside eatery. Both sides of the road were lined with rocky hillocks that ran in a zig-zag manner. The eatery was a stand-alone establishment; not many shops were nearby. Behind the eatery lay vast fields. Even on one side, there was a field. The other side was a grassy area where a cart was parked. Two cows sat under a tree, chewing the cud contentedly. The sun glittered down, and I felt at peace with the entire scenery. I looked around to take in more of the view until breakfast was served. I saw a pair of slippers lying carelessly near the cart. But what caught my attention was a rectangular wooden plank, worn and uneven, precariously balanced on an uneven stone. It seemed so unstable as if the slightest breeze could tumble it to the ground. I wondered how long it would stay balanced before it fell.

Soon after breakfast, we continued our journey. Around noon, we reached the village. The sight of the rural surroundings lifted my spirits. I felt a mix of anticipation and apprehension as we approached the house. My friend's Uncle and Aunt warmly welcomed us. After tea, Uncle showed us around. The house was a single-story building, showing signs of ageing. Cracks ran through the walls, and paint had peeled off in many places. The house needed repairs. However, one side of the house was renovated. The uncle informed us that it was done by his son, who worked in Mumbai. Though the house had ample space, it had an air of neglect. Like the house, the front garden also needed tending. An old man sat in the garden whom I was introduced to as the grandfather.

Later, we had a delicious lunch. The vegetables tasted authentic. During lunch, the Aunt again spoke about their only son, who lived in Mumbai. She said he funded the renovation of the house. With a proud smile, she added that he had always been a responsible and caring son, ensuring their comfort even from afar. I could see the glint of pride in both Uncle and Aunt's eyes. The grandfather sat quietly and ate his lunch with us.

In the evening, my friend and I went for a stroll to visit the village market. I asked my friend to tell me more about our host's family. She said the grandfather used to work in the village primary school. He had significant family liabilities. The Uncle was his only son. After completing his studies, Uncle tried his hand at business, which unfortunately did not succeed. The family mainly depended on the grandfather's meagre income. During his employment, the grandfather built the house by taking loans from various sources. My friend added that the grandmother was an enterprising woman who supplemented the family's income by weaving baskets for local vendors. The grandmother passed away three years ago. The financial situation slightly improved over the last two years after the grandson started earning money.

During dinner, the conversation again veered around the couple's son. Both Uncle and Aunt were full of appreciation for him. They said he understood his responsibilities at a young age and was sharing the family's financial load. "He is like a pillar of this house," Uncle said proudly. Grandfather sat quietly and ate.

The next day, I decided to spend some time with the grandfather. I went to his room, which required urgent repairs. He was sitting on his bed, listening to the radio. His face lit up when I told him I wanted to spend some time with him. He pointed to a rickety chair near the bed. Slowly, he opened up to me. I felt that he had not been listened to in a long time. I requested him to narrate his life's journey. How did he muster the courage to build the house despite financial constraints and family liabilities?

Grandfather's face lit up as he shared his story. He said he and his wife were determined to have a roof over their heads. Though they struggled hard to keep the family afloat, they held on to their dream of building the house. Purchasing land and constructing the house was a big decision, but he always felt supported by two sources: God's grace and the desire to leave the house to his son.

His face became sad at one point, and his voice softened as he continued, "I thought that our financial troubles would ease once my son grew up and started earning. But that did not happen. My son was unwilling to take up a stable job, preferring to try his hand at business. Since my daughter-in-law was educated, I suggested she join the village school, but she preferred to stay home. Until her last day, my wife contributed to the family's income by weaving baskets". The grandfather heaved a deep sigh before continuing, "My remaining days will pass away. I was destined to live a life of hardship. But I am glad my son and daughter-in-law will not face similar struggles. Their son will provide for them". With that, the grandfather fell silent. The room grew heavy with his unspoken pain. I bent down, touched his feet for blessings, and quietly left the room.

The next day, we thanked our hosts for their hospitality and started our journey back. They urged us to visit again during their son's holidays so we could meet him. The two days in the village were refreshing, a soothing escape from the rush of daily life. I felt thankful to my friend for persuading me to join her.

During the drive back, I sat silently, lost in thought. My mind wandered to the conversation with the grandfather and the unmistakable pride on the couple's faces whenever they spoke about their son. Then, unexpectedly, out of nowhere, the image of the unstable wooden plank which I saw in the roadside eatery popped into my mind. I could see it vividly—the rough edges of the plank, its surface worn smooth by time, wavering on the sharp edge of the stone. It seemed so fragile, so vulnerable to the slightest gust of wind. The memory stirred something profound within me.

In the days following the trip, during quiet moments, especially in the stillness of the afternoon, I would remember the grandfather's face and his life. He was the plank of the family, providing strength, support, and stability. It occurred to me that during our entire stay, the couple never acknowledged the grandfather's foundational support and his role in keeping the family afloat. I wondered if life might have been different for the grandfather had his son and daughter-in-law understood their duties towards him. Their pride in their son's financial support contrasted with their lack of gratitude for the grandfather's sacrifices.

Perhaps the Uncle and Aunt's oversight stemmed from years of financial stress and their habit of focusing on immediate relief. With their son's support, they finally had a chance to breathe. Yet, this narrow focus blinded them to the grandfather's cornerstone actions. The renovation of the house resembled climbing a ladder—easy when the lower steps are steady. However, failing to note the foundational steps risks climbing to the higher steps.

Building and modifying something is easy when we already have groundwork. Creating a foundation and building upon it requires courage. Revamping a house is far simpler than buying land and constructing a house amid financial struggles. For the grandfather, the house was not just a structure but his way of leaving a legacy. He had balanced his wooden plank by supporting it with unflinching faith in God's grace and a burning desire to secure his son's future.

It is very easy to unbalance the planks of our lives with our flawed perspective regarding duty and responsibility. We often expect others to own their responsibilities while ignoring our duties towards them. If we reflect upon our lives, we will see that much of what we build upon was initiated by someone else. We enjoy the shade of trees planted by others with a sense of entitlement. We do not appreciate the roles others play in our upliftment and advancement, whether in personal or professional life. But we are quick to take credit for our contribution.

Gratitude and acknowledgement may not change others' lives, but they profoundly impact our own. Admitting the grandfather's role might not significantly change the grandfather's life, except for the quiet satisfaction of being appreciated. However, it would transform the Uncle's understanding of his duty as a son and a father, enabling him to balance his plank. Without accepting and recognising the lower steps, climbing higher becomes unstable. Without gratefulness for others' efforts, our lives risk becoming like the unbalanced wooden plank, where a slight wind in the form of adversity can topple everything.

Have we ever wondered what areas of our life resemble an unbalanced plank?

Chapter Five

The Windchime

It was a marketplace in a hill station. We had come on a trip to the hill station for a few days to unwind and celebrate. My daughter's examination had just concluded, and we were eager to relax and enjoy quality time together. We could see a small shop from the corner of the road with handmade artefacts and decorations hanging from wooden beams. She wanted to buy a windchime—a simple object that promised calm and serenity with every gentle breeze. It would be a keepsake from the hill station, a cherished memento of our vacation.

The shopkeeper was an elderly man with a warm smile. His shop was filled with windchimes of every shape and size, each producing a distinct melody when touched by the wind. We examined many windchimes, running our fingers over the delicate metal rods and polished wooden chimes. Finally, we selected a beautifully crafted windchime made of bamboo and metal. He appreciated our choice and said, "Most people think windchimes only make music when the wind blows," he began, picking up the chime we had chosen. "But the truth is, they have an inherent sound, even when there is no breeze." He gently tapped one of the metal pieces with his finger. A soft, resonant tone filled the air, delicate yet profound. "You see," he continued, "the windchime does not need the wind to sing. It holds its own melody, its voice. The wind merely amplifies it."

My daughter smiled, pleased with the interaction. On the way back, she said, "These days, I find it so strange to wake up in the morning and realise I have no specific routine to follow, no portions to complete, no mood to manage." I understood what she meant. The last two years had been arduous for her. She had been preparing for the Joint Entrance Examination (JEE), the gateway to the country's premier Engineering Institutes. There were two phases of the examination: the JEE Mains and the JEE Advanced. She had set her sights on gaining admission to one of the top five IITs in the country. Admissions to IITs are through JEE Advanced. We had mentally prepared her for the formidable journey ahead, emphasising the sacrifices she would need to make regarding personal time, family gatherings, social events, and other pursuits she had previously enjoyed.

She was ready and excited to start the journey, her eyes full of resolve. She attended a full-time regular school and opted for online coaching classes instead of joining a full-time Coaching Institute. Her reasoning was sound; she wanted to fully participate in regular school's extracurricular activities and social growth opportunities. We supported her decision.

As days turned into months, the journey became uphill. School demanded attendance, assignments, projects, and tests. Being a meritorious student, she had a good standing in school, which added pressure to perform well in school tests. To make matters more challenging, she was selected for the Student Council and appointed Head Girl of the school. She embraced the responsibility gleefully, seeing it as an opportunity to represent her school in various forums. But the balancing act was, to say the least, gruelling.

The JEE preparation demanded immense mental stamina, grit, and determination. Completing the journey was itself a monumental task, let alone excelling. For students, the preparation for entry into any professional course comes during the peak of teenage years, a time of emotional turbulence. As parents, we resolved to provide her with a supportive, non-judgmental environment. We were aware of the potential pitfalls of the journey and the impact they could have on her mental health if not handled sensitively. Stories of students succumbing to the immense pressure of competitive examinations that abound in the media were heartbreaking. After all, each child's life is a world in itself, and the loss of even one is a tragedy of hundred percent.

As the journey progressed, we watched our daughter transform. A determined, purposeful gaze replaced the tender look in her eyes. As she adjusted her lifestyle, her perspectives evolved, and her tenacity grew. She began to value resilience and self-management. With our input, she adopted coping mechanisms to maintain a calm state of mind. We constantly urged her to take a holistic view of the process, emphasising that life was much bigger than any competitive examination or institution. The outcome of any competitive process depends on many factors, and effort is one of them. Academic achievements are important, but they form only a part of the life equation. True fulfillment requires courage, perseverance, and facing life's stark challenges head-on.

When the day of the JEE Mains examination arrived, she appeared calm, as if offering her efforts to the divine invisible force. She cleared the examination with flying colours. More than happiness, she felt gratitude for passing the examination.

"Many students must have worked as hard or harder. Luck and other factors also play a role," she said. Her maturity struck us.

In the JEE Advanced phase, she doubled her efforts. Meanwhile, she excelled in her Class 12th Board examinations, making her school proud. This preparation phase was more intense, akin to a cricketer in the 90s needing unwavering focus to score a century. Finally, after the challenging period, the examination day arrived. She emerged satisfied, saying she had done her best and would leave the rest to God.

As we awaited the final results, she spent time reconnecting with friends and indulging in family moments. She tried her hand at culinary skills while we pampered her with her favourite meals. We knew these moments were fleeting, as she would soon leave for college. The results came, and while her rank was commendable, it was not within the cut-off for admission to her dream Institute. Initially, my daughter was disconsolate. Seeing her good performance at the first attempt, the suggestion of taking a drop year arose from certain quarters. We were hesitant. Statistically, many successful candidates were droppers, but the uncertainties of another attempt and many other factors loomed large.

My husband and I were caught in a whirlpool of "what-ifs" and "should-haves." I felt a range of emotions within me. We had always emphasised focusing on the process rather than the outcome, yet here we were, grappling with doubts. The tension in the house was palpable, though my daughter had regained her composure by then.

One evening, we decided to let her choose whether to opt for a drop year or not. After all, it was her journey. We asked her to take a day and decide so that the process could be completed. The next evening, when I returned from work, I found her sitting quietly, absorbed in a mystery novel. We approached her. She calmly set the book aside and said, "I have decided." My heart skipped a beat. I was unsure which decision would make me happier, so I searched her face intently, trying to discern what was coming. Her expression gave nothing away. She was calm and composed, like someone standing at the midpoint of a road, able to see both directions clearly.

She began, "When I started this journey two years ago, I did not know much about what lay ahead. I had no idea what the path would demand from me. I might have been overwhelmed by fear and lost my balance if I had known. But I took it one day at a time. Each day brought new challenges—not just academic but also in terms of resilience and self-management."

"As time passed, I realised that the skills I built each day became the building blocks for the next. Every day showed me that I was capable of more than I had thought possible. Initially, I used to obsess over the result: *What if I succeed? What if I fail?* But gradually, I found that focusing on the day's tasks instead of the outcome eased my anxiety. My attention shifted from the end goal to the journey itself."

"This journey taught me so much about myself. In fact, I found myself through this process. Looking back, I have no regrets. I gave my best at every step. I do not regret attending regular school because the relationships I built with my friends and teachers are precious to me. I do not regret attending online classes, as they allowed me to focus on my progress rather than getting caught in unhealthy competition."

She paused briefly before continuing, her voice steady and reflective. "When embarking on a journey of this magnitude, having a goal is essential. It gives us direction and keeps us motivated to endure the daily grind. But as the journey unfolds, it can become so meaningful that the initial goal no longer feels as significant. That is what exactly happened to me."

"I discovered so much about my potential and myself along the way. Though the idea of taking a drop year is tempting, it would not add to my growth as a person. It would only serve to satisfy external expectations and affirm my potential, which I have already come to recognise."

"The JEE journey will always hold a special place in my heart. It has anchored me and will continue to guide me through future challenges, especially when the road ahead is unclear and self-doubt or fear creeps in. Though not in my dream institute, I have already secured a seat at another premier institute. I want to move forward. I am ready to begin a new chapter," she concluded solemnly.

Her words hung in the air, filled with wisdom and clarity far beyond her years. I looked at her with pride, knowing that this decision was hers alone, shaped by a journey that had not just tested her abilities but also revealed her true strength. At that moment, I recalled the words of the old shopkeeper: "The windchime does not need the wind to sing. It holds its own melody." My daughter has discovered her inherent music. The winds of time will only amplify it.

In life, we are all like windchimes, holding a unique melody within, waiting to be discovered. The inherent sound represents our innate potential, creativity, and capabilities. Through life's events, challenges, opportunities and encouragement, the breeze stirs our potential into action. However, the absence of the breeze does not negate the existence of the music within.

It is merely waiting for the right moment to resonate. In the same way, even if we have not encountered the right opportunities or support—our potential still exists, quietly waiting to be revealed and nurtured. Our intrinsic worth is not dependent on external validation. All it takes is the right moment, the right mindset, and the courage to nurture what is already within us.

Are we ready to recognise and acknowledge our inner melody?

Chapter Six
The Motionless Windmill

The plan was instantly made. Enough of this monotonous life! This time, we will make it happen! Four of us will travel to Hampi and spend a few days there, away from the hustle and bustle of city life. "I hope, like last time, we do not cancel the trip at the last minute due to some flimsy reason", I quipped. "No, this time we won't", assured Aditi. "Even if they cancel (she pointed towards Reshma and Ritika), both of us will go", she said in a voice full of determination. Reshma and Ritika objected in unison, "Why should we cancel? It is just that last time, an important assignment came up in the office". The tone of their voice was unconvincing.

We have been planning a trip for the past one year. Every time the topic came up, we would give reasons and say firmly, "Next time, we are going to make it, come what may." This time, after weeks of careful planning, things fell into place. All arrangements for travel and accommodation were made. We had been extra cautious because we did not want the trip's cancellation burden to fall on any one of us.

One early morning, we started on our trip. Once we started, our mood transformed. We left our tensions behind, and I could feel a sense of excitement. The relief of making the trip happen was palpable, and we felt jubilant. We passed through the bustling urban outskirts and entered the serene landscape that mirrored our spirits. The roads were well-maintained, making the journey smooth and pleasant.

The scenery changed dramatically as we neared Chitradurga, about 200 kilometres from Bangalore. On both sides of the road were barren, rocky hills. Hundreds of towering white windmills, with their graceful blades, stretched across the horizon like sentinels of the wind. The rugged, boulder-strewn hills and the sleek, modern structures of the windmills created a surreal atmosphere. It was an enchanting experience. I had never seen so many windmills at a time. The sun shone brightly, and the windmills stood still against the vast horizon, their blades motionless. They seemed almost lifeless, as though waiting for the winds to breathe energy into their motion.

We reached Hampi around noon. It is a UNESCO Heritage Site in Karnataka. It is a site of ruins, boulders, and the remnants of a once-thriving empire, the Vijayanagara Empire, one of the most influential and prosperous empires in Indian history. It was the capital of the Vijayanagar Empire. The site is dotted with intricately carved temples, ruins of palaces, markets, and water structures displaying architectural marvels. Despite its historical importance, Hampi is far from a bustling tourist hub. The place was not at all crowded, and its tranquil surroundings, with vast expanses of rocky terrain, offered a sense of peace.

On reaching the hotel, we immediately went out for sightseeing. Walking through Hampi, we felt like we had entered a bygone era. We imagined ourselves being transported to the time of the Vijayanagar Empire, walking through the markets where once precious gems were traded. The ancient feel of the site, the natural surroundings, and the stillness of the place put us in a reflective mind. The day passed beautifully, and we felt thoroughly relaxed.

The next day, as we wandered through the ruins, our conversations grew more profound, and one by one, our bottled-up emotions started pouring out. In the evening, we sat on the steps of the

Virupaksha Temple, the grandeur of the past surrounding us. The quietude of the place had a strange effect—it seemed to peel away the masks we all wore in our daily lives. We all started sharing our struggles.

Reshma started sharing her story…

Her voice broke with frustration and weariness as she said, "Sometimes I feel like I am carrying the weight of the world on my shoulders. Just yesterday, my son came home with his exam results, and they were… well, let us say they were not what I expected. His results would have improved if only his father had stepped in and supervised his studies. But no, it is all on me—his studies, extracurricular activities, everything. And on top of that, the office is a nightmare. I try my best to keep everyone happy— my boss, team, husband, and son—but no matter what I do, it is never enough. At home, they say I am too demanding. At work, I feel unappreciated. It is like I am failing everywhere."

Reshma paused, her eyes clouding with emotion. We waited patiently, sensing there was more she needed to say. She continued, lowering her voice, "You know what is strange? I feel like I am two different people. I am calm, professional, and even nurturing at work with my team. But at home… it is like something snaps. I find myself barking orders, treating my husband and son like subordinates. And then I hate myself for it."

We felt the emotion behind her words. Reshma continued in a reflective tone. "Maybe it is because I feel so unappreciated. I pour everything into my work and family, yet I feel invisible. My husband says I don't give him enough attention. My son says I am always stressed. But how can I not be? I am juggling a million things, and I get no help. If only people at work were more competent and my family helped me more, my life would be perfect."

Ritika leaned forward and asked, "Have you shared how you feel with your family?" Aditi added thoughtfully, "Could you delegate more at work or spare some time just for yourself? Sometimes, prioritising self-care is the only way to avoid burnout." I gave her my perspective. It seemed that everybody was disappointing her. Focusing on others' inaction can feel overwhelming. I asked her what would happen if she shifted her focus inward and took small steps to appreciate herself and rediscover the things that bring her joy.

Reshma sighed, her shoulders slumping slightly as she absorbed our words. "Ritika, I have tried talking to my family, but it always ends in arguments or silence. They don't seem to understand, and I feel worse." She glanced at Aditi with a faint smile. "Delegating at work sounds great, but trusting anyone to do it right is hard. It feels like more work to train someone than to do it myself." Then, turning to me, her eyes softened. "Appreciating myself… I don't even know where to start. It feels like everything I do is tied to what others need from me. How do I even find joy when I don't have little time for a break?" Reshma paused, looking down at her hands. "I know something needs to change, but I feel so stuck. It is like I am in quicksand, and the more I struggle, the deeper I sink."

We all kept quiet. Then Aditi took a deep breath and started sharing her story…..

"You know," she began softly, "sometimes we don't realise how much of ourselves we have lost until life forces us to stop and look hard. Sitting here with you all, I can't help but think about the pieces of myself I have let slip away over the years." She paused, her voice steady but tinged with emotion. "You all know me as someone who has always believed in my independence and ability to face life head-on. But life has this uncanny way of challenging the things we think define us. That is exactly what happened to me."

Aditi hesitated momentarily, her voice softer, "After completing my studies, I pursued a career of my choice with confidence and passion. I enjoyed travelling. Soon, I married the person of my choice, but within a few years, the relationship ended. When it ended, I thought I had lost everything. But I also believed it was a chance to rebuild, to start fresh. I found a new job, moved to a new city, and even met someone who seemed like he was everything I had ever hoped for." She paused before continuing, "Avinash was kind, thoughtful, and seemed to understand me in ways I had not experienced before. When we married, I thought I had finally found my footing again. But as time passed, I realised there were layers to him I had not seen—or maybe did not want to see."

Her voice wavered slightly, but she pressed on. "You see, Avinash grew up in financial hardship. So, he is very cautious about money. At first, I thought his frugality would go away with time. But over the years, it started to feel… controlling. Every small decision—every little thing I wanted for myself—seemed to need his approval. Financial independence, which I had worked so hard for, was slipping away. And the worst part? I let it happen."

She paused again, letting her words settle. "I convinced myself that I was keeping the peace for the sake of our family. But deep down, I started to feel like I was losing pieces of myself. The person I used to be was fading into the background." Aditi's voice grew defiant. She said she often wondered whether Avinash subtly took advantage of her past experiences. She could not shake the feeling that he might have sensed her hesitation to confront issues, thinking she would avoid rocking the boat given what she had gone through earlier. His subtle manipulation of the situation made her feel as though her desires were secondary to his control. Over the years, Avinash has tightened his grip on their money.

"What is the point of being financially independent if I have no say over my desires?" she confided. "I feel like I am constantly battling for the freedom to live my life." Aditi paused, her voice filled with sadness. "I have been playing along because I don't want to rock the boat. It is not just my life; it is about my son, too." But then, her frustration resurfaced, her voice growing stronger. "Am I meant to live like this forever? Can't I have a single wish of my own? I worked so hard to build a career and gain financial independence—just to be suffocated by someone else's control?"

Then, her voice became rueful. "What am I teaching my son through my actions? Later, he will start expecting the same behaviour from his partner as he sees me behaving. I feel so guilty for not standing up for myself. What should I do?" Aditi wrung her hands helplessly, the weight of her emotions overwhelming her. We sat, listening to her, each feeling a deep discomfort, silently grateful not to be in her situation.

Reshma gently asked, "Don't you think strength should also include standing up for your needs?" Ritika pointed out, "Financial independence is about choice, not just earning money. You seem to have let that choice slip away because you think you must adjust. Think about what you are teaching your child through your words and actions. Show him that it is okay to set boundaries and value yourself." I told Aditi she was brave enough to be honest with herself and us. I reminded her that Avinash's control does not define her. She could start discussing the subject with him, sharing her feelings openly, not to blame, but to express her views.

Aditi listened to us with tears welling in her eyes. Our words seemed to reach a part of her that had long been silenced.

Now it was Ritika's turn.....

Ritika sighed deeply, "Do you ever feel like you are just... stuck? Like no matter how much you achieve, it is never enough?" We were taken aback. "Stuck?" we asked in unison. "How can *you* feel stuck?". Ritika had what many would call a "perfect life". She was a corporate professional with a secure career, a loving husband who was financially sound, and a lovely daughter. From her early years, she had been ambitious. She excelled academically, landed a coveted job, and confidently climbed the corporate ladder.

"I know I should be grateful for my achievements", Ritika continued. "But I can't understand the feeling of a void within me. I keep comparing myself with my college friend, Puja. We were very close in college. We had similar dreams and goals. But now, she earns more than me, travels the world, and lives this glamorous life. And here I am, stuck in this routine—work, home, family. When I see her posts and photos on social media, it is like I live in her shadow.

"My husband often senses my dissatisfaction but does not understand it. He gets frustrated when I bring up these things. He thinks I have no gratitude, and maybe he is right. But it is not that I do not appreciate what we have—I feel like I am falling behind. Like I am not living up to some invisible standard. I don't know. Sometimes, I think it is not about Puja or anyone else. Maybe I am just... empty inside. Like I have been chasing things that do not even matter. And now I am stuck in this cycle of comparing, envying, and feeling miserable", Ritika ended with tears in her eyes.

Reshma spoke gently but firmly, "It is okay to feel that way. You are human, and we all compare ourselves at times. But the issue is how you measure your life. You are not stuck—you have just forgotten to celebrate your own journey. Maybe it is time to stop chasing external validation and ask what success means to you." Aditi added, "Social media makes it easy to fall into comparison, but you have so much to be proud of". I asked Ritika whether her feeling of being stuck could be an opportunity to reinvent herself. After all, life is not only about ticking boxes but also about growth, joy, and passion. Maybe it is time to explore what excited her without worrying about anyone else's journey.

Ritika listened intently to our words. She wiped her tears, took a deep breath, and said no more.

As the sun dipped below the rocky hills of Hampi, the air was heavy with introspection. The ancient ruins resonated with unspoken thoughts, urging us to share our stories. Then, I decided to share my story, my voice trembling slightly, carrying the weight of years of suppressed desires.

"I have always been a dreamer," I began, looking at the crumbling stones that had withstood the test of time. "From as far back as I can remember, I wanted to create something of my own, to build something that reflected my passions and values. I dreamt of being an entrepreneur, travelling the world, meeting people, and making a difference. But... life had other plans."

The others listened intently as I continued.

"When I graduated with a professional degree, my family, like most families, wanted stability for me. They wanted to see me in a secure, respectable, and predictable career. And I followed their advice. It was not a bad decision; it just was not my decision." "I have been in this career for years, and it looks like I have done well on paper. Promotions, appraisals, accolades—everything that should make someone feel accomplished. But it does not make me feel that way. Over time, I have realised that my job, though stable, has become monotonous. It is like running on a treadmill—constant movement but going nowhere. I am growing professionally, but I am not growing as a person. And that, more than anything, torments me."

I paused, letting the silence speak for a moment before continuing.

"My real passion lies elsewhere—in helping people unlock their potential. Over the years, I have quietly built up my skills in this area. I have read, trained, practised, and grown. And I know, deep in my heart, that I can make a real difference in this field. But the thought of leaving my current job terrifies me. It is not just about me—my family, finances, and the fear of failure. I think about the steady paycheck, the stability, and the security I have built, and I feel torn. At the same time, my entrepreneurial desires have become almost haunting. The voice within me does not let me sleep, constantly whispering that this is not where I am meant to be."

I took a deep breath, feeling the emotion swell in my chest.

"Every day, I feel this restlessness growing inside me. It is like being caught between two worlds—one that is safe but stifling and another that is risky but full of promise. I do not want to wake up one day, years from now, and regret not taking the leap when I had the chance. But then, I think about the consequences. What if I fail? What if I am not as good as I think I am? These questions keep me awake at night, and the fear of the unknown paralyses me."

The ruins around us seemed to echo my inner turmoil. I looked at my friends, their faces filled with empathy and understanding. As I finished, the stillness of Hampi enveloped us. The ruins seemed to whisper their own wisdom. My friends offered their thoughts, encouragement, and perspectives. But more than anything, they gave me the space to voice my fears and dreams—to hear myself out, to confront the restless spirit within me. At that moment, I realised that the answers would not come all at once. But sharing my story with my friends was the first step toward clarity.

That evening, as we walked back to the hotel, we shared an unspoken understanding—a sense that we had crossed an invisible threshold. The weight we had carried in our hearts for so long felt lighter, as if the ruins of Hampi had absorbed our struggles and whispered back silent insights.

After reaching the hotel, we sat on the balcony, the cool breeze carrying the distant hum of crickets. Each of us was lost in thought, yet there was a calmness, a collective sense of healing. "Do you remember the windmills we saw on the way here?" I asked, breaking the silence. The others nodded, their expressions softening. "They stood so tall and majestic, but they were not moving," I continued. "Initially, I thought they were just idle, useless without the wind. But now, I see them differently. They were not stationary; they were waiting. Waiting for the right breeze to set them in motion."

Reshma leaned forward, her voice thoughtful. "It is strange, isn't it? We are so much like those windmills. We have all this potential, but we let ourselves stay still, blaming the lack of wind instead of realising we can create our own." Ritika added, "I kept thinking my happiness depended on the 'winds' of success and travel of others. But maybe it is not about waiting for the wind. Maybe it is about being ready to move when it comes and appreciating the stillness in between." Aditi, who had been quietly listening, spoke up. "I have been stuck for so long, depending on others to turn my blades. Maybe it is time I stopped waiting and found my own way to move my inner windmill."

We all looked at each other, the windmills suddenly taking on a profound meaning in our shared journey. As we turned in for the night, there was quiet excitement in the air. Deep in our hearts, we felt that Hampi would bring something special tomorrow—a sign, a realisation, a moment of clarity. Each of us carried a new hope as if the ruins of the past we had explored today had permitted us to rescript our futures.

That night, as I lay in bed, I thought about how Hampi, with its ruins, had given us a space to share, to be vulnerable, and to heal. We all drifted to sleep with the same thought in our hearts—that tomorrow would be a new beginning, a day when the winds might finally blow, and we, like the windmills, would be ready to move.

The next morning at Hampi dawned gently. The air felt different—lighter, as if the burdens we had shared the previous day had been lifted, leaving room for clarity and hope. There was a quiet determination in each of us, an unspoken promise that today would be the day we began to move forward.

As we wandered through the stone-carved temples, Ritika spoke first. "You all were right," she admitted. "I have been so focused on what I do not have that I have lost sight of what I do. I guess I have been letting comparison steal my joy. I need to redefine success for myself, not based on what my friend Puja or anyone else is doing but on what makes me happy. Maybe this emptiness is not bad—it is just a signal that I must pause and reassess what truly matters to me." Her words resonated deeply, and we could see the spark of resolution in her eyes.

Later, as we sat by the riverbank, Reshma shared her thoughts. "Yesterday's conversation made me realise how fixated I have always been on other people's flaws. I have been demanding from everyone—my family, colleagues, even myself. I can't change other people, but I can definitely change how I respond. I will start by asking for help instead of expecting it. I will involve my husband and son more at home, not as subordinates but as partners. At work, I will delegate with trust instead of resentment." Her voice carried a newfound calm, and we could sense her inner storm settling.

As we climbed a hill to watch the sunset, Aditi took a deep breath before speaking, her voice trembling but steady. "I don't even know how to thank you all," she said, her tone a mix of gratitude and vulnerability. "Hearing your perspectives made me realise how much I have been holding inside. This fear of rocking the boat is suffocating me. I have been so scared of losing what I have that I have not stopped to think that I have already lost my voice, happiness, and sense of self. It kills me to think that I might be teaching my son to expect this kind of dynamics in his own relationships someday. I want him to see that his mother is strong and can stand up for herself even while loving and caring for her family. I have been so focused on what I can't do that I have forgotten what I *can* do. Maybe you are right—it does not have to be a battle. Maybe it can start with a conversation. Even if it is hard and does not go the way I hope, at least I will know I tried." It was clear that Aditi felt a spark of hope and determination within herself for the first time in a long time.

The sun dipped below the horizon, casting a warm glow over the landscape as if urging me to express my thoughts. I said, "For years, I have been standing still, afraid to leave the safety of my job and chase my passion. But Hampi has taught me something important. These ruins—once grand and powerful—still stand tall despite the passage of time. They remind me that even if I stumble, I will endure. I have decided to take the leap and start my journey as an entrepreneur. I do not want to live with regrets anymore." My friends smiled, their support giving me the courage to believe in my decision.

The next day, as we drove back to Bangalore, the sight of the windmills greeted us once again. The blades were moving this time, catching the breeze and spinning gracefully. We stopped to admire them, and Aditi said softly, "They are finally moving. Just like us." Ritika added, "They remind me that even in stillness, there is potential. And when the winds come, we must be ready to turn." Reshma smiled, "It is like they are showing us how to adapt, flow, and harness our strengths." I felt a wave of gratitude wash over me. We saw them motionless, and now we see them moving. It is a reminder that life has its seasons. The key is to trust the process and be ready for the winds of change.

As the windmills disappeared from view, they prompted us to reflect on our untapped potential and how we hold ourselves back. Through our own resistance, we stall the blades of our inner windmill, preventing progress and growth. Yet, these windmills impart a profound lesson: patience and readiness are essential for seizing the right opportunities or conditions. Inactivity does not always mean wasting time. It can be a meaningful part of a larger cycle, offering moments for renewal and preparation. True wisdom lies in recognising that not every moment calls for action. The windmill reminds us of the importance of balancing motion and stillness, encouraging us to align our efforts with life's ever-changing winds.

The trip to Hampi had been more than a journey through history—it had been a journey into ourselves. We returned home with a renewed sense of purpose and gratitude, ready to face the challenges ahead with courage and hope. And just like the windmills, we were ready to turn, move, and embrace the winds of change that life would bring.

How can we let our inner windmill turn freely, knowing when to move forward and when to pause, trusting both are needed for our growth?

Chapter Seven

The White Snake

The atmosphere hung heavy with unspoken tension. An icy stillness enveloped the room, signalling the onset of something inevitable. I had already sensed it. The uneasiness loomed like dark clouds, pressing down on all of us.

"I don't want to go to school tomorrow," declared my fifteen-year-old daughter, her voice carrying an unusual finality. I understood the underlying reason. Tomorrow, the marks from the recently concluded examination will be distributed. Mathematics was the culprit.

I recalled the day of her Mathematics exam. When I asked how it went, she said, "Fine". The level of "fineness" was about to be revealed. Over the past few days, she had been subtly preparing us with remarks like, "I think I am not going to score well in Maths," and "This time, my marks might be worse than last time." I understood that she was trying to manage our expectations. I decided not to respond, choosing instead to let the storm pass without engaging too much in her feelings or my own growing anxiety.

My maternal instinct wanted her to excel in all subjects, but I knew she needed space to navigate her emotions. A bright and diligent student, her name often ranked among her class's top achievers. Teachers appreciated her sincerity and creativity. Her marks are often a reference point for others.

Yet, beneath her academic success and the praise she receives, my daughter has an inner world that she keeps carefully hidden. She guards her feelings closely, like an oyster sheltering its pearl. Over the years, she has perfected the art of non-communication as a defence mechanism. Despite our parental lectures on the "benefits of openness," she prefers reticence. But today, at breakfast, she came out of her shell just enough to state her intention of skipping school. I decided to respond. "It is important to know where you stand so you can improve for your Board exam," I reasoned. "Besides, some of your friends might also have struggled with the exam. You must know how to deal with such situations," I lectured. A little voice in my head retorted, "Did you know how to deal with low marks when you were fifteen?" I ignored the voice, brushing aside my own hypocrisy. The annoying voice has a tendency to emerge at the most unexpected moments.

The day dragged on, her anxiety becoming more palpable. She withdrew further into her shell, her thoughts swirling like a storm. I sensed that we were approaching the eye of the storm. That evening, she made one last attempt. "Can I not go to school tomorrow?" she pleaded, her eyes welling with tears. My heart ached. Why could I not say, "Okay, stay home. Collect the answer papers later." This would immediately ease the situation, and the tension would dissolve. She would be happy, and I would feel relieved. Just then, the persistent voice inside my head whispered: "Will that really help? Will that make her grow in the long run?" This time, I decided not to ignore the voice. I realised that avoiding the issue was not the solution. I needed to understand her deeper fears.

I sat her down beside me. "Tell me the real reason," I said gently. She hesitated. "You don't want your friends to know your marks?" I ventured. Her silent tears confirmed my suspicion. The real struggle was not about marks but the fear of her carefully built image being shattered.

I remembered my moments of vulnerability when my fears felt insurmountable. There were times when I had let go of countless opportunities—like the chance to take on new projects or step into leadership roles—to avoid the discomfort of being judged. I had turned down invitations to speak at events or share my ideas, convincing myself that staying in my comfort zone was safer than facing potential failure or judgment. It was easier to stay in the background, where the risk of being exposed seemed smaller, even though deep down, I knew these missed chances were keeping me from growing.

I realised that dismissing her emotions would not be helpful; her feelings were real and needed to be acknowledged. Ignoring them would only deepen her resistance. With care, I explained how she could handle the situation, hoping my words would reach the innermost corner of her mind beyond her resistance. Even after a while, I did not get any positive response. I knew guidance has its limits—it is the individual who must take the final step. Finally, I concluded by saying, "The choice is yours. Do what serves you best."

The next morning, I waited silently. She got up, dressed, and boarded the school bus without a word. Relief washed over me. Tears of gratitude filled my eyes as I whispered, "Thank you, God." Turning to my husband, I said, "Our daughter has won. She has faced her white snake moment." My husband was amused. He asked, "What is a white snake moment?" The term had slipped out unconsciously. Reflecting on it, I began explaining about white snakes and their symbolic meaning.

White snakes are rare in nature, and their lack of camouflage makes them defenceless. Their inability to blend into their surroundings makes them highly susceptible to predators, so they are not commonly found in the wild. These snakes are often found in captivity. Their unique appearance can be seen as a symbol of exposure and fragility—qualities often associated with vulnerability in life. Yet their lack of protection also sets them apart as extraordinary and symbolises hope and renewal.

A "white snake moment" in life symbolises moments of weakness, which leads to transformation when confronted and managed effectively. It is the moment of shedding old identities, beliefs, or behaviours to embrace growth. At this time, making the right choice can feel exposing and intimidating. We all face such situations in our journey through life. These are the times when we must let go of self-created images and beliefs that no longer serve us. Often, the fear of judgment or rejection keeps us from stepping into these instances of growth. But just as a snake sheds its skin to grow, we, too, must shed old layers to reconnect with our true selves. We must realise that these white snake moments hold immense potential for development, self-realisation, and a deeper connection to our authentic selves.

When my daughter returned from school, I sensed her joyful mood. Although she indeed scored low in Maths, as we had anticipated, her happiness stemmed from the victory of confronting her fears. She had stepped beyond the safety of comfort and chosen maturity instead. I silently saluted the courage in her young heart. It was not the absence of fear that made her brave but her willingness to face it head-on, embracing the discomfort of imperfection.

I realised that this experience, though seemingly small, would become an anchor for her in future moments of uncertainty. Whenever life tested her resolve, she could look back on this day and remember that progress is not about flawless results but about daring to take the step, even when the path feels uncertain. As she grows older, she might laugh at her teenage fears. But she will also remember the strength of facing them and the rewards of choosing inner transformation.

We all have our "white snake moments." Do we confront them, or do we shy away?

Chapter Eight
The Sunlit Cave

It was early January. The world outside was shrouded in dense fog. The fog had blurred the line between sky and earth, turning everything into a uniform grey. Nothing seemed visible at first glance—except for a bunch of vibrant red flowers on a tree in the neighbour's garden. Their colour stood out boldly, defying the monotony.

As I gazed out, my thoughts began to wander. What if the fog never lifted? How would we adapt to such a world? My musings were interrupted by an unexpected thought: "When it is dark, you can light a lamp. But what do you do when it is foggy?" The question lingered, teasing my mind.

Just then, my phone rang, pulling me back to reality. It was my friend, a voice from years of shared memories. Our friendship had weathered time and distance, becoming a comforting constant. Though we did not speak often, we had an unspoken understanding that allowed us to pick up right where we left off.

Over the past few years, my friend has been navigating a series of personal challenges. Her parents' declining health had consumed her time and energy, and the recent loss of her mother had left her reeling. She was deeply attached to her mother, and the void felt insurmountable. Her father was frail and required constant care. She often described her days as a relentless cycle of caregiving and grief, with no space to process her emotions. Today, her voice carried an extra weight of despair. "It is as if I am stuck in a cave. It is all gloomy everywhere," she exclaimed. "I don't know if I will ever find my way out or if I am doomed to stay in the cave forever."

I listened as she poured out her heart, sharing the latest twists in her life. I tried to offer words of encouragement, but I could feel the enormity of her pain. It is not easy to guide someone out of their inner turmoil. I wished I could do more, but I knew we must walk our own healing journey. As we ended the call, I glanced outside. The fog had lifted, and the morning sun bathed everything in golden light. My spirits rose with the sight, and quiet gratitude filled me for the clear, sunny day. Yet, a question lingered: "Can we be thankful for a sunny day outside while feeling foggy inside?"

The day unfolded with its usual rhythm, but my thoughts kept returning to our conversation. In the afternoon, as I stood on the balcony, my eyes caught the same red flowers I had noticed in the morning. They had been visible even in the thick fog. My friend's words echoed in my mind: "It is as if I am stuck in a cave." Her words resonated deeply, and I realised how they captured a universal experience—the cave phases of life.

I recollected a trip to a hill station years ago, during which I visited a deep cave in the forest. The cave was mid-sized, its entrance concealed by natural boulders. Inside, it was dark and still. At first, the darkness was impenetrable, and we could see nothing. Slowly, as our eyes adjusted, faint outlines emerged. It was as though the darkness could never fully deny the sun's quiet determination to illuminate, no matter how hidden or unreachable a place seemed. The tourist guide explained that caves serve many purposes. Some are sanctuaries for seekers of spiritual enlightenment, while for wanderers and trekkers, they serve as shelter against wild animals and harsh weather. Each person's relationship with the cave depends on their need or perspective.

Reflecting on life, I realised we all encounter "cave phases." These are periods of darkness, guilt, shame, and self-doubt. During such times, the mind is clouded with fear and uncertainty. It is easy to feel stuck, disconnected, and overwhelmed. We question the meaning of life, our achievements, and our choices. After the loss of a loved one or a major life change, we may retreat into ourselves to process our emotions and find clarity. These are the cave phases of our lives— periods of introspection and solitude.

In a natural cave, the presence of light depends on its structure and depth. In the same way, in the cave phase of our life, the presence of inner light depends on our state of being. Our awareness of this light determines how we navigate these phases. Do we adopt the mindset of a trekker who has been forced into the cave and longing to escape or a sanyasi (sage) who has embraced the cave as an opportunity for growth and self-discovery?

A trekker forced into a cave by external circumstances often focuses solely on escape. The darkness and confinement feel unbearable, and the longing for the outside world creates inner chaos. The mind becomes a breeding ground for negative thoughts: "What if I am stranded forever?" "Why is nobody looking for me?" "No one cares."

These thoughts form a web, trapping the trekker in a cycle of despair. Even if the external danger passes and they come out of the cave, the negative mental patterns remain, turning the world outside into an extension of the cave.

In contrast, a sanyasi sees the cave as a place to retreat from external distractions and seek self-discovery. Accepting solitude, they use the stillness to meditate and reflect. Over time, their inner chaos quiets, and clarity emerges. This mindset transforms the cave from a place of darkness to one filled with an inner light. When they leave, they carry with them newfound wisdom and strength, ready to face life's challenges with a renewed perspective. In this way, they turn a normal cave into a 'sunlit cave'.

The 'sunlit cave' represents a phase of introspection, personal growth, or transformation but with an optimistic or enlightened perspective. This is a time of healing from past wounds and struggles when we learn, grow, and discover newfound strength. Unlike the darkness and isolation typically associated with caves, the 'sunlit cave' is illuminated by clarity, hope, and understanding. The light within this cave represents the insights and understanding that emerge from deep reflection. The 'sunlit cave' reveals valuable truths about self, purpose, and direction—even in times of withdrawal and solitude.

As I reflected on these mindsets, my thoughts turned to my friend. Her struggles had forced her into a cave of her own, a place of retreat and shadow. Could she shift her perspective and find the light within that darkness? Will she turn her cave into a 'sunlit cave'?

Much like that morning's weather, life's foggy moments eventually clear. Perhaps my friend needs a gentle reminder of the red flowers visible even in the densest fog—a symbol of hope and faith. Next time we speak, I will remind my friend to look for her red flower. After all, even in the darkest caves, a sunlit glimmer is always waiting to be found.

Are we willing to turn our caves into sunlit ones, trusting that light is always waiting to be discovered?

"The quiet spark is always waiting,
ready to illuminate the path
when we dare to look within."

Chapter Nine

The Lion Cub In Wilderness

The dining table discussion veered toward the places to visit when my friend Swati and her daughter, Rhea, came to stay with us. My daughters were excited as Rhea was of a similar age. They quickly made a long list of places. I reminded them that although our guests would be here for a week, the first two days would be occupied by the competition in which Rhea had come to participate. Undeterred, my daughters added even more suggestions to the list. Among them, I voted for Bannerghatta National Park.

Since childhood, I have always been fascinated by zoos. The animals, with their unique characteristics, amuse and intrigue me. Yet, it had been years since my last visit to the zoo. Life, with its endless priorities, had taken over. Choosing the zoo was not just about the animals; it was a way to reconnect with a cherished memory. Swati and I had spent countless hours at the zoo during our college days, bunking classes and talking endlessly. Perhaps, unconsciously, I wanted to relive those carefree moments, reconnecting with my old friend through the shared nostalgia of our favourite hangout.

Swati and I had been inseparable in college. She was vibrant, outgoing, and always ready to take on challenges. We used to affectionately call her the 'Lion Cub'. Life had taken us in different directions after college. Though we kept in touch through occasional messages, they were not enough to bridge the gaps that life had created. I was thrilled when Swati called to inform me about her visit to Bangalore for her daughter's competition. This was an opportunity to reconnect and catch up on everything we had missed.

Swati and her daughter arrived the next day, and the kids gelled instantly. Their camaraderie gave us the space to talk and share. The days flew by in a whirlwind of visits to malls, museums, and parks. By the fourth day, as planned, we set out early for Bannerghatta National Park. We knew it would be a full-day affair.

Bannerghatta National Park has a diverse collection of mammals, reptiles, and birds. Our visit began with the safari ride, an experience that never fails to captivate me. Observing animals in their naturalistic settings evokes a sense of adventure and awe. The meshed vehicle added an air of suspense as we ventured deeper into the jungle. We saw a majestic tiger lounging lazily on a rock, its bored expression betraying an indifference to our presence. We saw a lioness playing with her cubs while a lion sat apart, seemingly uninterested in the frolic. The lion, often regarded as the king of the jungle, embodies strength, courage, and leadership. Yet, this lion appeared contemplative at that moment, as if grappling with a deeper truth. Watching the cubs play, I wondered whether a lion cub would be able to thrive in the wilderness and fend for itself after living a sheltered life in the zoo. The question lingered, a poignant reminder of the delicate balance between nature and nurture and the challenges of reclaiming one's innate strength in unfamiliar terrain.

After the safari, we walked through the enclosures, marvelling at the animals. Hundreds of photographs were clicked, and we silently thanked the digital camera inventor. In the afternoon, we found a shady spot in the children's park to enjoy our packed lunch. The kids wandered off, allowing Swati and me to reminisce about our college days. "So many things have changed," Swati said suddenly with a sigh. Before I could say anything, the kids returned, and we set off for home.

That evening, after dinner, Swati and I retreated to the terrace garden. A gentle June breeze rustled the leaves, and the warm light created playful shadows. Swati seemed unusually quiet. Over the past few days, I had noticed clouds of worry on her face. The Swati sitting beside me was not the same confident friend I had known. Many things have changed for her.

I gently asked, "What is bothering you?" Swati could not hold back anymore. Tears streamed down her face as she poured out her heart. "I can't take it anymore. Why has life turned out this way for me? Your life seems so perfect. You are financially independent, you have a wonderful husband, and everything seems to have fallen into place for you. Look at me. On every side, I see nothing but problems."

I waited patiently, understanding that this small opening would lead to the larger story she had been holding inside. The Swati before me was a shadow of her former self—she had forgotten her inner strength. Like a lion cub yet to grow into its strength, my friend seemed to be waiting, unsure of her power and purpose.

Swati began recounting her life since college. She was married off soon after completing her studies, even though she had always believed she was destined for great things. Her parents, however, had different plans. They did not encourage her to pursue a career, firmly believing that a "good boy" with a steady income was the ultimate key to her happiness. Swati chose to trust her parents' vision.

At first, life seemed smooth. Her husband had a respectable job, and Swati dedicated herself to managing her new home. Her parents, especially her father, remained a constant pillar of support. He often reassured her, "Why should you work when your husband earns enough? Focus on your family." Swati did not resist. While she occasionally felt a pang of regret watching her friends excel in their careers, she convinced herself that her parents were right. "A stable marriage is better than the unpredictability of a job," she often told herself.

For years, this arrangement worked. Her husband's income and occasional financial support from her father kept the household running—not lavishly, but comfortably. Swati found joy in her role as a homemaker, pouring her energy into raising their two children. Over time, she noticed her husband's drinking habit, but she chose to ignore it, praying that it would not worsen. Her father's presence acted as a safety net, shielding her from financial and emotional strain.

The first blow came five years ago with the sudden death of her father. Swati lost not only a beloved parent but also her anchor. Her father had been her emotional and financial lifeline, and without him, she felt lost. She missed his unwavering support and wise counsel every single day.

The second blow struck a year ago when her husband was diagnosed with a serious illness. His health declined rapidly, and with it, their steady income vanished. Swati now faced mounting school fees for her children, escalating medical bills, and everyday expenses, all of which became an unrelenting source of stress.

Swati felt utterly overwhelmed. Beyond the financial strain, the emotional toll of caring for her husband pushed her to her limits. She directed her anger and frustration toward her parents, blaming them for the life she was now trapped in. "Why didn't they insist I build a career? I was capable enough. Why did they marry me off so quickly? Was I just a burden to them?" she lamented.

Her frustration did not stop there. She also blamed her husband for neglecting his health and shirking his responsibilities. "Why didn't he think of us? Why did he let his habits ruin everything? Now, I am left to deal with everything alone," she said angrily, her eyes brimming with tears. "I feel like my life has been ruined because of choices others made for me. When I see my friends and relatives who have careers and financial independence, I can't help but feel they are so lucky."

I sat silently, listening intently as Swati poured out her heart. I had not realised it was already 11:30 p.m. Her words revealed a deep longing for the comfort of her father's guidance and for the days when her life felt shielded from harsh realities. After some time, Swati glanced at the watch and said, "It is late; let's go. I think it was God's hand that brought me here. I needed this outlet." I gently mentioned that she could have brought her son, but she explained, "Someone has to stay with my husband; he can't manage alone." Her response reflected the weight of her responsibilities and the sacrifices she continued to make for her family.

The next day, I woke up unusually early after a restless night filled with disjointed dreams. My mind was still processing everything Swati had shared the previous evening. Seeking solace, I settled quietly on the balcony. It was quiet, except for the occasional flutter of a bird. There is something uniquely clarifying about mornings. Perhaps the promise of a new day, brimming with possibilities, opens our minds to fresh perspectives.

In the stillness of the morning, I realised that Swati's life resembled that of a lion cub—blessed with innate strength and potential but never given a chance to develop independence. Shielded by an overprotective father, she never learned to hunt or fend for herself. Her father, though loving and well-meaning, assumed the roles of protector, provider, and problem-solver, preventing her from confronting life's challenges. His constant sheltering, though rooted in good intentions, left Swati unprepared for the world's harsh realities. Despite possessing all the qualities needed to thrive, she was never encouraged to build resilience or problem-solving skills.

Her father, believing his primary role was to spare her from hardship, handled every obstacle, ensuring her comfort. He never pushed her to pursue a career, thinking that financial security through marriage was all she needed. However, this well-intended protection became a cage that stifled her growth and kept her from stepping outside her comfort zone. Like a lion cub raised in captivity, Swati grew up in an environment where all her needs were met effortlessly, leaving her untested in adversity.

When her father passed away and her husband was diagnosed with an illness, Swati was suddenly thrust into the 'wild' for the first time. The secure environment she had always known vanished, leaving her unprepared to face the responsibilities that now fell on her shoulders. Like a lion cub unexpectedly released into the jungle, Swati panicked. Perhaps this led her to blame her father for sheltering her too much and her husband for neglecting his health.

I realised that Swati was struggling to take control of her life, often looking to her parents and husband for explanations about her circumstances. Even though her father passed away five years ago, she has not yet taken the steps to pursue a job despite having the qualifications. I wondered what might be holding her back.

Achieving financial independence comes with its challenges, and the comfort Swati sees in her friends' lives is the result of hard work. They sacrificed personal time, committed to their careers, and faced many struggles along the way. Swati, on the other hand, had embraced the role of a homemaker, a role though fulfilling, has its own set of challenges.

Blaming others never solves problems; it keeps us trapped in them, fuelling feelings of frustration and resentment. If Swati wants to change her situation, she has to take responsibility for the role she has played. Even if she feels she had no choice in the past, she must recognise that her journey is far from over. The instincts and strength of a lioness are still there within her. But years of dependence have dulled her ability to recognise or use them. She must step out of her comfort zone, accepting the challenges instead of fearing them. Just as a lioness becomes the protector of her pride, Swati can rise to become the anchor for her children. With courage, effort, and self-awareness, she can awaken the lioness within and learn to survive and thrive in life's wilderness.

That day, I found Swati in a different state of mind. She appeared to be in a pensive mood, with a distant look in her eyes. The outburst from the previous day and the release of long-held emotions had a calming effect on her. Over tea, I shared the insights from my morning reflection. At the end, I told her, "Your journey is not over. Though you have faced hardships, you still have the strength to rebuild. You have always been a lion cub. It is not too late to rediscover your claws and thrive."

Swati listened quietly, her expression softening. For the first time, I saw a glimmer of hope in her eyes. The lioness within her was beginning to stir. A sense of realisation seemed to wash over her as if she was finally acknowledging her own power. I knew that change, however gradual, was already taking root. The lion cub would eventually find its way into the wilderness.

How can we navigate the wilderness of our own journey, trusting that, like the lion cub, we will find our way and discover our strength along the path?

Chapter Ten

The Stiff Grass

The train raced forward, the rhythmic sound of the wheels against the tracks providing a comforting backdrop to the hum of my thoughts. Seated in my berth, I glanced at the elderly lady sitting opposite me. She appeared to be in her late sixties, her posture poised, a newspaper unfolded in her hands. From the way she arranged her things carefully, I surmised that she was accustomed to order and control.

Usually, I would have passed the time by watching the trees blur past the window or diving into a new book, but today was different. Despite the mystery novel waiting patiently in my handbag, I felt no inclination to read. Something about the moment's stillness made me turn my attention to the lady before me. My inner sense told me that a far more interesting novel was sitting before me, waiting to be unravelled.

After a while, I broke the silence, politely asking, "Aunty, are you travelling to Delhi?" Of course, the train was bound for Delhi, and I immediately chided myself for such a foolish question. I quickly rephrased, asking if she planned to go to any hill stations afterwards. She smiled, replying that she would remain in Delhi.

We exchanged pleasantries, and soon, the conversation shifted to her life. She began to share her story - a tale of hardship, resilience, and sacrifice. Due to her unsettled family life, she faced tremendous challenges raising her two children single-handedly in dire financial conditions. She spoke with high emotions, fully immersed in the moment. The image of a dam came to my mind—once opened to release the river's flow, there was no holding it back. Though she spoke with pride about how her sacrifices had shaped her children's success and independence, there was an undercurrent of bitterness, as if she was still carrying the weight of those years.

As she spoke, it became clear that her self-perception was deeply tied to her role as a mother. Her life's narrative revolved around the idea that everything good that happened to her was because of her efforts. She seemed trapped in a cycle of self-importance, as if she were the central character in a story where everyone else revolved around her.

"That person was good because he liked me," she said, or "I wanted things to happen this way," or "Because of me, this worked". She saw every success in her life through the lens of her influence, and she could not imagine these things happening independently of her. At the gentle mention of God's invisible hand, she gave a brief nod—less in agreement and more as a cautious acknowledgement, as though wary of tarnishing her image in my eyes.

It struck me that she was oblivious to the possibility that the world could exist outside of her influence, that people might be good for their own sake, or that circumstances could be favourable without her orchestration. Her identity was so tightly interwoven with everything around her that she could not see beyond herself. Her colleagues were good because they respected her; her relatives, who had looked down on her, were the antagonists in her story.

Yet beneath the surface, there seemed to be a quiet struggle. At one point, her voice softened, and I could see a fleeting line of worry on her face. She explained that her children have grown up and now sought independent lives. Though they acknowledged her crucial role in their upbringing, they yearned for freedom from her constant involvement. This seemed to trouble her deeply, as if she could not reconcile their desire for space with her belief that their success was entirely due to her sacrifices. She could not understand why they sought a life free from her influence because she had "made" them who they were.

As she continued, I noticed how exhausting it was to listen to her. The constant "I, me, myself" narrative drained me. It was not just her words but the weight of her worldview that left me feeling heavy. She seemed unable to perceive anything beyond her perspective. It was not that she was unaware of the world beyond her. Rather, she seemed to be caught in a constant pull between her desire to be seen as the architect of everything good in her life and allowing life to unfold.

I wondered if her struggle was about denial or about finding balance and integration. Denial would mean refusing to see the changes around her, particularly her children's growing independence and their need for autonomy. Instead, her conflict seemed to be about integration—accepting and reconciling these new realities with her sense of self. As a mother who had sacrificed and shaped her children's lives, it was difficult for her to embrace the truth that they were now independent individuals with their own desires and choices.

Finally, after two hours of hearing her recount her triumphs and grievances, I excused myself, citing a need for a nap. As I lay down, my mind wandered to mundane tasks awaiting my return from Delhi: the leaking tap in the kitchen, the wildly growing grass in my garden, and countless small chores that always seemed to pile up.

As I drifted off to sleep, the image of my garden came to mind. Most of the grass was lush, green, and soft, swaying gracefully with the wind. But there was one stubborn patch where the blades had turned yellow and grown stiff, standing rigid and brittle against the breeze. This patch resisted the care I lavished on the rest of the garden, refusing to soften despite water, sunlight, and fertiliser. I remembered asking the gardener about it, and he had said with a knowing smile, "Sometimes, the soil underneath becomes too compacted, not letting the roots breathe. You have to loosen it and let in air and water. Only then can it thrive again."

Later, when I woke up, I saw that the lady was on the phone, speaking with her son. The conversation was peppered with unsolicited advice –"Do this, do that." She ended the call with what seemed to be a subtle reference to me, saying, "I am having a good time. She is enjoying talking to me." As I listened, the image of the stiffened grass returned to my mind, and I reflected on her life.

In her youth, the lady had likely been like the soft, adaptable grass, bending gracefully to life's challenges with resilience. Raising two children alone, enduring societal judgment, and battling against adversity would have required much strength and courage. Yet, somewhere along the way, that flexibility seemed to have hardened. The sacrifices she had made, though admirable, had led her to a place where she no longer bent or adjusted. Instead, she stood rigid, anchored in her sense of entitlement to control the lives of those she had nurtured. She has grown like stiff grass, with her emotional soil hardened and unresponsive to the needs of others.

Her words reminded me that resistance often conceals deeper, unspoken needs. I sensed her silent yearning for validation, recognition of her sacrifices, and an unspoken fear of losing her place in the story she had so carefully constructed. The weight of her self-importance seemed both a shield and a burden, protecting her from the vulnerability of letting go yet holding her captive to a narrative that no longer fit the evolving lives around her. She appeared to be stuck inside her story and perception.

The train continued its journey smoothly, and the lady, despite her rigidity, remained warm and engaging. She was well-versed in politics, religion, and philosophy, and I learned much from her views on these subjects. The next day, as the train pulled into Delhi station, her son was waiting to receive her. She proudly introduced him as "my son", emphasising the word "my". I smiled politely, but at that moment, I could not help but think of the stiff grass in my garden.

While reflecting on stiff grass, I realised how easily rigidity can creep into even the most well-meaning actions. I recalled my conversation with my young daughter a few days back when she had felt uncertain and vulnerable (her white snake moment). The source of her anxiety was that she did not want to face her friends, especially after getting low marks in Mathematics. The fear of letting go of the image she had carefully maintained in front of her friends, of being seen as less than perfect, weighed heavily on her.

At first, I had held on to the idea that my words could break through her resistance, much like the stiff grass standing firm against the wind. I tried to offer solutions, thinking they would ease her worries, but I noticed her hesitation growing as I spoke. My attempts to guide her felt like they were pushing against her emotional wall. Her feelings were real to her, just as real as the wind is to the grass. I was so focused on solving her dilemma that I had forgotten to acknowledge the emotional weight she was carrying. Instead of bending to her needs, I firmly believed that providing solutions was the best way to help. I was like the stiff grass - unyielding, unable to sway with the wind of her emotions. Unknowingly, I had stifled her emotional growth by not allowing her the space to confront her vulnerabilities.

In a moment of realisation, I had chosen to step back and let go of my need to direct her. "The choice is yours. Do what serves you best," I had said, softening my stance. It was an act of bending, offering her the space to find her answers. This shift was not passive; it was an active choice to trust her ability to navigate the situation.

This experience profoundly reshaped my perspective on flexibility. I had always seen adaptability as external—an ability to adjust to circumstances or solve problems. But this moment showed me that true flexibility begins within. It is about being able to adapt not just to the situation but to the needs of the people we care about. It is about bending to their emotional landscape rather than forcing our ideas of what is best.

Like the wind gently bending the grass, sometimes the most powerful thing we can do is allow ourselves to yield—to soften our approach and enable others to navigate their paths. Like the soil under the stiff grass in my garden, we too can loosen the soil beneath us, letting in air and water to nourish our roots and allow us to thrive in the face of life's challenges. After all, resilience is not resisting the wind but learning to sway with grace.

In which areas of our lives are we exhibiting rigidity, like the stiff grass resisting the wind?

"Rigidity preserves the known,
but only flexibility unlocks new possibilities."

Chapter Eleven

The Lost Casino

As I walked through the opulent casino halls during a trip, the gleaming lights, the clinking of coins, the shuffle of cards, and the whirl of the roulette wheel created an atmosphere of possibility and anticipation. People come to the casino hoping to win big, yet each spin, roll, or hand is tinged with uncertainty.

The tables were not just about cards or dice; they were stages where the drama of human lives unfolded. The stakes were not always money but dreams, fears, and identities. Observing the players, I was reminded of the people whose stories shaped my journey—each grappling with their own 'games' of life.

Near one of the blackjack tables, I noticed a man, probably in his mid-forties, dressed in a dark suit. His demeanour was calm but focused, starkly contrasting with the young man beside him, who fidgeted nervously with his chips. As the dealer dealt the cards, the older man maintained his composure, occasionally glancing at his cards and making measured decisions. The younger man, on the other hand, hesitated, over-analysed, and frequently changed his mind. When the older man finally won a significant hand, he smiled, collected his chips, and walked away, leaving the young man visibly more agitated.

Curious, I approached the older man as he sipped his drink at the bar. Striking up a conversation, I asked him how he remained calm under pressure. He smiled and said, "It is not about the cards you are dealt but how you play them. You cannot control the hand you are given, but you can control your response. The key is to know when to hold, when to show, and when to walk away. Same as in life."

His words resonated deeply. Every decision in the casino, much like in life, is a gamble. Players often try tilting these odds in their favour through strategies, fallacies, or sheer persistence. Similarly, in life, our perspective can limit us or expand our possibilities. For example, the young man at the blackjack table was paralysed by his fear of losing. He could not see that each hand was an opportunity to learn and grow. His focus on avoiding loss prevented him from taking the risks necessary to win. In contrast, the older man's calm appearance reflected his understanding that losses are an inevitable part of the game.

In a casino, what sets the winners apart is not merely luck—it is their resolve, their ability to take calculated risks, and their courage to face uncertainty. These qualities allow them to turn their "lost casino moments" into winning moments of opportunity for transformation.

Reflecting on the stories I have shared in this book, I realised how life often feels like a casino. Each individual enters the casino of life with their unique set of chips—their talents, resources, and circumstances. Their beliefs, desires, and fears influence the games they choose to play and the risks they take. As I contemplated on the lost casino moments of the characters in my stories, I pictured how we encounter such moments in our own lives.

Sometimes, we act like stiff grass, resisting the winds of change and refusing to yield. In our white snake moments, we cling to old identities, beliefs, or behaviours that no longer serve us. Sometimes, we embody the sinister otter, masking our true intentions behind a façade to manipulate situations or pursue self-serving goals. By doing so, we gamble away opportunities for genuine connection and renewal. We forget that we are windchimes having inherent melody and become overly dependent on external forces, like the wind, to create music in our lives.

We create lost casino moments by unbalancing the planks in our lives when we fail to acknowledge the vital roles played by others in our growth and advancement. We overlook the quiet power of sincerity and alignment with a higher purpose when we measure our worth by the magnitude of our actions and forget to live in balance.

Lost Casino moments occur when we resist the winds of change, unwilling to turn the blades of our inner windmill and generate the energy needed for progress. We try to predetermine the outcome of our actions, forgetting that life, like a five-sided dice, is unpredictable and multi-faceted. By choosing not to roll the dice out of fear, we miss opportunities to explore possibilities and discover new outcomes.

Our lost casino moments are when we fail to recognise our inherent strength, like a lion cub who forgets to sharpen its claws for the challenges of the wilderness. In such situations, we neglect to see the light glimmering in the darkest caves, dismissing the wisdom of approaching life's trials with a sanyasi mindset—a spirit of detachment, focus, and acceptance.

Every game in a casino relies on a mix of luck, strategy, and risk-taking. Similarly, life presents us with endless opportunities to roll the dice or place a bet. The results of our choices—whether loss or gain—depend on the actions and intentions we invest in them. Just as a different bet in a casino would yield a different outcome, the decisions we make in life shape our paths in unique ways.

As I left the casino, I could not help but think about the symbolism of the place. Each game, each player, and each bet mirrored the complexities of life. The lost casino is not a physical place; it is a state of mind where we lose sight of our inner resolve and courage. It is the moment when we allow fear, arrogance, or self-doubt to dictate our actions. But the casino also holds the promise of rediscovery. Every spin of the wheel, every roll of the dice, and every shuffle of the cards is a chance to start anew.

The stories in this book, like the games in the casino, remind us of the choices we face and the power we hold to shape our destiny. Life will always have its uncertainties, its moments of triumph and despair. The key is to approach life's peaks and valleys with the wisdom of the seasoned player—one who knows that the game is not just about winning or losing but about playing with integrity, resilience, and an open heart.

The Lost Casino is within each of us, waiting to be rediscovered, reminding us that the most excellent game we will ever play is the one we play with ourselves, and our best bet is the one we place on ourselves. The stakes are high, but so are the rewards. All we need is the courage to sit at the table and the resolve to play our hand to the best of our ability.

Our biggest jackpot is discovering the strength, wisdom, and possibility that we carry within us and knowing that every moment has the potential for transformation as long as we are willing to play.

Are we ready to enter The Lost Casino and discover the power of betting on ourselves?

"The treasures of life are not always in plain sight;
sometimes, they wait behind
the doors we fear to open."

Acknowledgements

Writing *The Lost Casino* would not have been possible without the incredible people who have inspired, guided, and walked beside me on this journey.

I sincerely thank my husband, Prashant, for his steadfast support, love, and encouragement to chase my dreams. My heartfelt love goes to my daughters Monal and Ana, whose courage and resilience inspire me daily and remind me of the strength within us all.

I am grateful to my parents, brother and family, whose blessings and love have been my foundation. Their faith in me has given me the courage to explore and grow. My heartfelt gratitude goes to my Uncle, whose unwavering support and inspiration have always encouraged me to dream bigger and strive for excellence.

I am thankful to everyone who has touched my life in big and small ways. Each interaction, each shared moment, has left an indelible mark on my journey.

I thank my readers for taking up this book and starting a new journey inward. Even if you take a single step to explore life's hidden possibilities, I would feel that the book has fulfilled its purpose.

Above all, I am deeply grateful to the invisible force that guides my path and fuels the fire of imagination. This force reminds me of the beauty of possibility and the power of trust.

* 9 7 9 8 8 8 9 6 9 9 9 1 2 6 *